The Hopeless Romantic

Poems of Love, Loss, and Desire

By

Marco A. Valdez-Blake

I0086699

1st Edition

Copyright © 2015 Marco A. Valdez-Blake

All rights reserved.

ISBN: 0692452451
ISBN-13: 978-0692452455

FOR SARA

I wrote many of these poems before we met, yet I never knew who I was writing for until I met you. I love you darlin.

Contents

Advice

About the Author

ACKNOWLEDGMENTS

Thank you to everyone that I ever showed any of my work to. My first social media site where I was given so much positive support for my work. My friends that pushed me to reach my dream when I brought the idea up. My dad for telling me about the list that will make me a complete man, this is one step closer. My mom for always understanding me, and always nudging me to follow my heart. And lastly, Sara, for being the reason I finally finished this book.

LOVE

KNOWING YOU'VE FOUND THAT SPECIAL SOMEONE

When your heart races
at the sight of them
When your palms get sweaty
right before you take their hand
When you can't speak as they talk to you
When you can finally talk
and you feel like you've known them forever
When your lips touch
and you don't want to stop
When all you need
is a kiss to cheer your worst day
When you make out and you stop just to kiss instead
and it turns out better
When your feelings are expressed
and you're not sure what they mean
When you're confused
and they make it all clear
When everything you see reminds you of them
and they think of you always
When you know you'd give your life
for that one person
That is when you know you've found them
That special someone
That you want to spend the rest of your life with.

HOLDING YOU

When I hold you
The world stops moving
When I hold you
I feel safe
When I hold you
I know

I have found what I was looking for all these years

You saved me
From the dark pit of loneliness

We met, and you ran your fingers through my hair
We met, and I saw my soul in your eyes
We met, and I knew

I know that now
I'm the happiest I've ever been
I know that now
You'll always be there

I know that
By just holding you
I can express myself as I am
I don't have to be someone I'm not
I can be the man you fell in love with

When I hold you
I know that we were meant to be together
When I'm holding you
I know how much

That I love you

My Heaven

You are always there
When I feel all is lost
When my heart is full
You are always there
When I am angered by everyone
When I am alone the world

You are always there
To share my memories
To bring back my smile

You are
And always will be
My Heaven

I Can't Express

I Can't Express
My love for you
The way I feel about us two.
You're the one,
I want to spend my life with.

The one who sees that my love is no myth.

These warm feelings I get when I see you,
the flips my heart makes when you kiss me, too.
I want to tell you how I love you so,
But my words can't express my feelings.

You are the one,
who lights up my darkest day.
You help me through life's parade.
And I will always know,
that I can't express,
my heart to you,
how I Love You So.

Love

Love
How I get through the day
Love
How I miss you every moment we're apart
Love
What I finally found in you
Love
I will always be true
Love
Our never ending passion for each other
Love
Our longing for one another
Love
How we get along so well
Love
How we enjoy every second together
Love
We will always have each other
Love

How you make me feel

This thumping in my heart
Is real
What I see when I gaze into your eyes
Is the promise
Of your love for me and your trust of me
You make my heart stop
Only to breathe long enough to beat faster
I am captivated by your beauty
I am held still by your kindness
I feel safe when I am with you
I feel warm in the cold when you hold me
I am yours

I am here for you
If ever you need a friend
I will always be here for you
As however you intend

I will be there when you cry
I will wipe the tears from your eyes
Just so that you stop feeling hurt
I would give anything
Just so that you never have to feel pain

All of this
Because you make me feel
In love

SINGING SOFTLY

Here I am
Softly singing
Of sweet caresses
And eyes that are all I see

I will hold your hand
Up to my face
And kiss it gently, so

You know how it is
I feel for you
And I can't, I won't let go

I am singing softly
Of words and kisses
Whispered in the night

Tears are shed
And wiped away
I'll be the one to clean your face

I'll mend your heart
And make you laugh
Just to see you smile

You are the day
You are the night
You are the beam, of hope in light
I'll follow you
Where there's no end in sight

Here I am
Softly singing
Of sweet caresses

Your eyes...
Are all I see

I Miss You

I want to kiss your frown away
Hold you until your sadness fails
Until warmth reclaims your bones
On a cold winter's night

You make my nights sweet
Relax my mind
Raise my spirit
And I miss it

I miss your touch
Your care
How you hold me safe
A haven for my secrets
You understand it all

Never judging
Never denying
Never lying
Always supporting
Always there

The way your mouth says
I love you
The your body says
I need you
I miss it

The embrace
Your skin against mine with my face in your hair
The curve of your back with my hand on your waist
Moving my forehead to touch yours
Desiring a kiss
From your lips so soft
I hope for the best

And while you're gone
I can't feel
I can't sleep
Without you next to me
I love everything about you
And become less of a man without you

I miss it all because
You are my everything
I miss you

LOVE

Love means nothing when you're not around
A broken mirror it falls to the ground
Whatever happened to your smiling face
Wrapped in my arms, I was saved by your grace

A smile you gave
Set me free to the world
As long as you were there
As long as I could hold…
Onto you and your warmth
Against the cold outside
I wouldn't, couldn't freeze
Against the dark night

You bring me to the surface
From the long dive down
And every time I see your face
I am reminded why I smile

GUESS

Can you guess
How I will live
When you're gone?

When I can no longer find comfort in your eyes?
When your smile can no longer light up my darkest
days?
When our hearts are separated by the tortures of
time and space?
When our lips can no longer meet in bliss...

WHEN THE FLOWER MEETS THE SUN

The sun rises above a grassy plain.
Wind flows,
Causing waves .

The flower takes a chance,
Peeking at the sky,
Testing the space
To bloom.

The sun looks down,
Watches the flower.
A dainty yellow rose
Is meeting his glare.

Roots take place
As the heat subsides.
Experience shows
This dance is no try.

As springs before
And summers to come,
The rose dances to her partner,
To bloom for the sun.

Though separated by space,
Confused by time.
Experience shows
That circumstance is all but a crime.

Taking the chance
To hold firm in her spot,
The rose decides to stay once again.
The sun welcomes her,
His favorite flower,
To the place she has always had.

Though fall and winter may wane her beauty,
His strength.

The sun and flower dance again,
For this is their time.

LOSS

Always

The nights
the days
the mornings
the evenings

the misunderstandings
the miscommunications

the gifts
the surprises
the realizations
the love

My breath was constantly taken away
My heart was given before I knew it was gone

My defenses shattered
My soul opened
to you
to us

Friends
the hardest thing to change
is to become friends

If this is what it takes for us
For you to stay in my life
And for life to go on

Then I will remember everything
With a smile on my face
A gleam in my eye

And I will know
That nobody can take away

My memories
My happiness

Not even myself
As hard as it is to try
I will
For you

Maybe one day
We can try again
I don't know if I will be here or not
But I will always be your Friend
And you will always be loved

Best Friends
Always

I'd Do It Again (For Better or Worse)

There aren't enough words to describe
All the different ways I felt inside
When you'd lean on me by your side

Everything we had was made of clouds
Of hopes and dreams and freedom, now

I'd do it again
No matter how hard it went
I wouldn't give up those memories
I hold them inside
No tears in my eyes
Because of them I'm who I'm meant to be

So
I'd do it again
No matter how hard it's been
Taking that next step
After we left
...each other

You were the highest point in my life,
And the slope since we cried
Our teary goodbye,
Has brought me close
...to failure

But I remember our smiles
The times we had
The good and the bad

I won't replace the life we had
The road we walked, the one we had

I'd do it again

Every moment we spent
Together for better or worse
I'd do it again
In a heartbeat
Because you meant that much to me

I am who I am today because of you
Remembering lessons learned
Remembering how I yearned
For you

I'd do it again
No matter how it went
Just so I could know what love felt like
I'd do it all over again
Given the chance
I'll do it again
Every time

Loss

How can you miss that which you gave up
Voluntarily be less
Than happy with yourself
Sad when she is not there
A smile taken
Yet given, away

Sunlight evades the heart with a hole
Or simply shines through
Expanding the slow
Painful lack of a whole-
Ness leaving the soul
Empty and wanting
Regretting that sole choice
To let go

Broken Heart

Paint me the fool
As the crevasse grows
Cracking the middle
As only true pain shows

I broke your heart once
And I shatter mine now
Lost after seeing you
Only once since our
Last kiss

I had no idea
That you felt so strong
No clue that my heart
Had beaten so wrong
To turn from your love
And hide like a child
For fear of a failure…
Of letting you down

I hit myself hard
For realizing so late
Over a year later,
More than anyone should take
To understand emptiness
And why it is there
A sick gaping hole
Filled with despair

I write as though you've died
Yet you are perfectly well
It is my soul that has perished
Without you
This is my hell

A heart broken in cruel joke of time
Of fear and frustration
Unwilling to cross the line
I sit here alone
Without you to hold
And my night becomes colder
My broken heart barely whole

THE SAME, THE CHANGE

Clouds rolling overhead
The sun breaking through
Showing the path to the heavens
A clear blue sky today
The sun warming my left side as it sets
Its the same place, the same spot
So much has changed
The trees are mostly bare with winters homecoming
The grass is much, much less greener
That hidden path, the place I sit now...
Is still there
The groove I sat in
I sit in now
The top of a small valley, where a pebble can start an avalanche
I see the trees that framed the horizon last time I was here
This time I see only their branches
It is very different here now, the second time
It was the best spot
I saw a clash in the sky
And two paths,
Going to the light...
...And to the infinite night
Everything I saw
Is gone today
It has been over a year I think, since I actually sat here
How time heals and hurts
Changes yet remains the same
The landscape is much different
Less special
But still unique
And wholly mine to remember

ANOTHER ROMANTIC SONG

The sky is dark
It shines so bright
Millions of sparks
Lighten the sky
And I'm
Looking at the stars
Looking up the great white stars

I look and wonder

Is she looking at the stars
Looking up at the same, the same stars
I walk, round, this
Beautiful town

Watching the stars
I hear the laughter of the people
The wind through the streets
It reminds me of the times
That she would look at me

And I'm looking at the stars
Looking up at the stars
Hoping that she's looking at the stars looking up at same white stars
Shining so bright
Like a fire in the night
Lighting my way
While I

Look up at the stars hoping she's
Looking up at the same white stars

Song for a Second Chance

Here is the last thing I wrote before I fell asleep
A memoir of thoughts left unseen
A note scribbled in the dark
Folded up and tossed away
Where do I start...

Day one left me out of breath,
A smile was all that you left
Laughing and joking until we cried,
Our tears a promise, I

Wrote this song for the nights I've missed
Lying next to you, I wish
I had a second chance

Through ups and downs
We can spin around,
Watching the stars in the sky.

A picnic here
A picture there
Memories meant for us to share. I

Wrote this song for the nights I've missed
Lying next to you, I wish
I had a second chance
To take your breath away, I can...

I can, I will!
I'll give you every thrill, I'll
Put the world in the palm of your hand,
A promise because I can

I've written this song for the nights to come
Lying next to you, I wish

I didn't need a second chance

To give you that first kiss...
To never have to miss...
The way you look with a smile on your face,
Dancing the night away. I've

Written this song just for you,
Lying here awake,
Without you I wish
For a second chance.

DESIRE

CHOICES

Things that make you want more
Life makes you want it
Makes you want it back
Things are understandable
And incomprehensible
The same time can mean so many things for so many different reasons
You must find your way
Your path is laid bare
If you but choose to see it
To allow yourself to enjoy it
It won't hurt you
It will only do unto you as you let it
So don't be afraid
Embrace it
Whichever path you like
Just take your chance
And be happy

Playing with Fire (Till the Burns Hurt)

Red and glowing
The heat is flowing
Through my skin

It rises inside me
A fire within me
That you have kindled

You move right with me
Our hearts entwined
Forever

Your lips on mine
Excite me in time
To burn

I'll touch the fire
Lay down, admire
Your every...move

Because touching the fire
And feeling the burn
Won't ever hurt
Enough to turn me...away

Wicked as the flames may be
They won't burn my heart
Making me yell
Making me tell you to stay

I'll touch the fire
That you ignite
Every time
You're in my sight

My hand caresses
Every inch of you
And the fire warms the touch

You smile at me
And say to me
That touch could make you melt

And I'll
Touch the fire
That you ignite
Every time
You're in my sight

It won't burn
As long as it's you
It won't burn

Your eyes are shut
You bite your lip
I kiss your neck
So you won't twitch

The fire rolls through
Warms me and you
The heat melts away the cold

Your eyes excite
A feeling inside
Igniting the fire
We can't describe

It won't burn
As long as its you
It won't burn

I'll touch the fire
That you ignite
Every time

You're in my sight
And come away unscathed

With you
The burns won't hurt

POEM OF INFATUATION

I would wander around
For nights at a time
To see your beauty
Lit by the moon's soft light

I would twirl your hair
Between my fingers
As it cascades down
Restlessly, sweeter

Are your deep dark eyes
Than a view of heaven
A glimpse of your smile
Is my inspiration,

You have me intrigued
You have me shaken
Where this desire comes from
Is long since abandoned
For fear of rejection
For want of acceptance

I count on my hand
The times I have seen you
And countless are they,
The times that I need you

Perhaps it is a fool's ideal
To let flow so freely
The emotions of a man
Locked away so deeply

I am not aware
Of how far they will take me
But you in my arms

It must be safely...

Caught up in your smile
Intent on your gaze
Laughing greatly
Escaping the maze
Of continued solace
Toward the strongest of phrase

I want you.

ROMANTIC SONG #1

If I could but give my heart,
My soul away
Piece by piece
It would fall into place
Each beat would thump
Each drum would roll
And I would stand
Above this hole
I will dance for this among the stars themselves
I will give for this my heart as well
I am out there,
Out here
I am
Love, I am
Adoring this chance
For something great
I will always be that champion freight
Forever, I will be there
Giving my heart
My soul away
Piece by Piece
Along the way

Romantic Song #2

Give me a reason to give my heart
Give me the strength to go so far
And I will
I will stand by you forever
I will stand though the earth shakes round me
I will hold you until forever
Though fires may burn around me
If you just
Give me the strength to give you my heart
If you but
Give me the strength to go so far
I will never let go
As long as you still want me
I will take each crippling blow
If you ask you will receive me
And everything I am
I will
Always
Love you
Forever
Love you
Just give me the strength

HERE IN YOUR ARMS

I look across the room
Watch your hair cascade down
Flowing like a river
Calling me out

Your eyes lock into mine
Searching for something
So I walk over to see you
Holding that one thing

In your arms
I will walk
Into your arms
I will hold on

Your fingers make circles in my back
Relaxing me softly
Tracing shapes of nothing
Wandering slowly

I kiss your face
Your cheek, your lips
Tracing my own shapes
I just can't miss

You fit into me
And I into you
As the fan circles above us
Giving the cue

Lost in this moment
Holding you close
Wandering, circling fingertips
Creating a prose
Of dimensional patterns

Not letting me go

Here in your arms
I will stay
In your arms
I will hold on
Tracing my name
With yours underneath
Meeting your lips
Which I can't release
As I hold on
Here in your arms

READ BETWEEN THE LINES

I'm writing a letter
Meant for specific eyes to see
Drowning the noise
With my thoughts not perceived

Each stroke of my pen
Every shape that I draw
Makes words worth expressing
Raw, I'm in awe

I remember your face
I remember the day
The look that you gave
Without an expression, in that random place

I see through your eyes
And I write what I saw
That piercing gaze
That put me in shock

You'll read between the lines
See a message in between
A hidden agenda
That's yet to be seen

Between the lines
Between each word
Lies a subtle hint

I'm writing a letter
For specific eyes to see
Scratching out my thoughts
For those eyes to read

That piercing gaze

That tore me apart
Saw through the facade
And read my heart

Between the lines
Between each word
Lies a song
Never meant to be heard

Between the lines
Between each word
Is the letter I write
My thoughts unheard

HEARTSONG

The heart wants
what the heart sees
what the heart feels

It is unmistakable
unshakable
and drives me ever free

Free of the shackles
of rules and limits
I forge my own path
marching over and through it

Mistakes are made
lessons are learned
Good and wrong
I take what I get
all that I deserve

I would have you
by my side ever more
A comforting presence
a softly opened door

That guards the locked box
holding my soul within
Because you are that
from which my heart begins

To tremble
to beat
to crave what I seek
Having you near me
is all that I need

My heart wants
what my heart sees
what my heart feels
So I may be free

My heart wants You.

The Final Temptation

Her sighs echo around my room
Her eyes flutter with every kiss
Her thighs twitch with every move

Moans trickle from her mouth

She grips air to keep herself steady
She stares into my eyes,
Passion circling in a whirlpool
She opens her mouth

"I love you" she cries

I know
So I give her what she craves
To make love
Unyielding
Desperate
Sweet
Caressing love

Now she claws on my back
Not realizing
That I feel nothing…
But the pleasure

Entering the one I make happy

Only after giving in
To the final temptation

As It Will Be

I would pull the moon from the stars
To but see you smile
Snatch a candle's glow
For just a while,
As you warm my heart with your sweet embrace
I'd give you the key
To unlock my cage.

One beat in my chest
One softly released breath
Is at it takes for you to captivate me

A smooth touch
A sharp pull
A shock between your skin and mine
As I realize what's mine is yours
And nothing more

You are a breeze in the wasteland that is this life,
An oasis in the desert of extreme,
And unbridled desire

I write this for you
Before I find you
So that when I know these feelings
I'll know it's you

Bright passion in a dark room
Cold in anger during summer's bloom
A balance of extremes in a dull, voided world
Igniting a fire,
Which could burn the water.

You'll know me and I'll know you

When the choice is taken away,
By two hearts consumed.

ADVICE

THE STRANGEST GIFT

Ripping
Churning
Squirming
In a cavity it's
Burning

Hot with emotion
In a swirling cold,
Dense block
Combusting from within
Pressure against pressure
A struggle to win

Conscious or unconscious
It happens regardless
Turmoil
Consistently spoils
Brings about new ideas
Brings out new hopes
Escaping the hole
That the charade replaces

There is always a front
Always a layer
To peel away
That makes or breaks her

No stopping

No quitting
Too close to care
How much it may change
How much can you care?

Make a decision
Choose a choice
Hold back
Or step forward,
Toward,
The path of disorder

It is familiar yet new
An incarnation that few
Recognize or comprehend
With the time that they knew

Always look up
When given this gift,
Even if you're unsure
Why it exists.

ABOUT THE AUTHOR

Marco lives in the Houston area within the great state of Texas. He lives with his beautiful love Sara, and their goofy dog Rockie. He holds a Bachelor's Degree in Music, with Voice as his instrument, and at one time taught the Classical Style of singing for 3 years. He has always held a passion for creative writing since his childhood. This is his first book, but hopefully not his last.

www.ingramcontent.com/pod-product-compliance
Lightning Source LLC
Chambersburg PA
CBHW031528040426

42445CB00009B/446

* 9 7 8 0 6 9 2 4 5 2 4 5 5 *